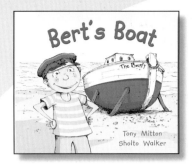

Walkthrough

Let's look at the
called 'Bert's Boat

Our book today
in it. Can you spo

P Phonic Opportunity

Discuss what 'rhyming' means and
share examples of some rhyming
words.

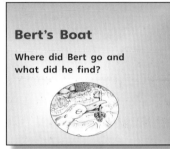

Bert's Boat

Where did Bert go and
what did he find?

Walkthrough

Let's turn to the back cover. Read the
blurb. Where do you think Bert might go?
What might he find?

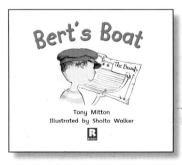

Walkthrough

Turn to the title page and read the title
again with me. Look at the picture. What
is Bert looking at? What do you think he
is going to do?

Walkthrough

This is Bert's boat. He built it.

This is the boat that Bert built.

2

Observe and Prompt

Word Recognition

(P) Encourage the children to use their decoding skills to sound out and blend the phonemes through each word.

● The word 'built' may not be decodable for children at this stage. If they struggle with this word, model reading it for the children.

Walkthrough

Do you think Bert is pleased with his boat? Would you like to sail in a boat like this?

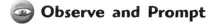

Observe and Prompt

Language Comprehension

- Do the children think Bert will sail in his boat? Where might he go?

Walkthrough

The sea looks a bit rough, doesn't it? Look at how Bert's boat bobs on the waves. (All bob up and down in your seats.) What can Bert see ahead of him?

This is Bert's boat.
It bobs on the waves.

Observe and Prompt

Word Recognition

(P) Check the children can sound out and blend the phonemes all through each word to read them. Can they find two words with long vowel sounds ('boat' and 'waves').

4

5

 Observe and Prompt

Language Comprehension

- Encourage the children to talk about the story and predict what may happen next.

Walkthrough

Who is Bert helping in the picture?

This is the bird Bert quickly saves.

6

Observe and Prompt

Word Recognition

Ⓟ Encourage the children to keep using their decoding skills to sound out and blend the phonemes in each word. If they struggle with 'bird', tell them this word. Can they find another word with the 'er' phoneme (Bert)? What differences can they notice in how these words are spelt?

Ⓟ Can children identify a word that rhymes with 'waves'?

7

 Observe and Prompt

Language Comprehension

- Check that children understand that the bird needed rescuing because it was trapped in a net.
- What do the children think will happen next?

Walkthrough

Where is Bert now? How do you think he's feeling?

This is a cliff with deep, dark caves.

 Observe and Prompt

Word Recognition

(P) Encourage the children to use their decoding skills to sound out and blend the phonemes all through the words 'cliff', 'deep', 'dark' and 'caves'.

Language Comprehension

- Do the children think Bert will go to the caves? What might he find there?
- Encourage them to read the text with appropriate intonation and expression.

Walkthrough

Where do you think the bird is going?
What do you think might be inside the box?

This is a box
that sits on the rocks.

The Bounty

👁 Observe and Prompt

Word Recognition

P Can the children identify the rhyming words on this page ('box', 'rocks')?

Language Comprehension

● Encourage the children to make predictions about what will happen next in the story.

Walkthrough

What has the bird got in his beak? Why do you think that he is giving this to Bert?

This is the key that opens the box.

12

13

 Observe and Prompt

Word Recognition

 Can the children find a word with the long vowel 'o' sound, like in 'boat'? Which letters make the 'o' sound in this word? (o/e)

Language Comprehension

● Check that the children can predict what Bert will do with the key and what might happen next.

10

Walkthrough

What's in the box? How do you think Bert feels now?
How would you feel if you were Bert?

And this is the gold
that Bert unlocks.

👁 Observe and Prompt

Word Recognition

P Ask children to break
'unlocks' into syllables
and sound out and
blend the phonemes
through each syllable
to read the word.

● The word 'gold' may not
be decodable for children
at this stage – if they
struggle, tell them this
word.

Language Comprehension

● What do the children think
Bert will do with the gold?

Walkthrough

Look at Bert and the bird. How are they feeling now?

Bert and the bird,
afloat on their boat.

The Bounty

16

 Observe and Prompt

Language Comprehension

● Check that the children can find two words with the long 'o'
  phoneme ('afloat', 'boat') and two with the 'er' phoneme
  ('Bert', 'bird'). Which are the rhyming words?